D1233338

AUG 1 5 2007

HU

Beavers

Diane Swanson

Gareth Stevens Publishing
A WORLD ALMANAC EDUCATION GROUP COMPANY

Please visit our web site at: www.garethstevens.com
For a free color catalog describing Gareth Stevens Publishing's list of high-quality books
and multimedia programs, call 1-800-542-2595 (USA) or 1-800-387-3178 (Canada).
Gareth Stevens Publishing's fax: (414) 332-3567.

The publishers acknowledge the support of the Canada Council for the Arts and the Cultural Services Branch of the Government of British Columbia in making this publication possible.

The author gratefully acknowledges the support of the British Columbia Arts Council.

Library of Congress Cataloging-in-Publication Data

Swanson, Diane, 1944-
    [Welcome to the world of beavers]
    Beavers / by Diane Swanson. — North American ed.
      p. cm. — (Welcome to the world of animals)
    Includes index.
    Summary: An introduction to the physical characteristics, behavior, habitat, and life cycle of beavers, emphasizing the development of beaver kits.
    ISBN 0-8368-3560-3 (lib. bdg.)
    1. Beavers—Juvenile literature. [1. Beavers.] I. Title.
QL737.R632S9   2003
599.37—dc21   2002030278

This edition first published in 2003 by
Gareth Stevens Publishing
A World Almanac Education Group Company
330 West Olive Street, Suite 100
Milwaukee, WI 53212 USA

This U.S. edition © 2003 by Gareth Stevens, Inc. Original edition © 1999 by Diane Swanson. First published in 1999 by Whitecap Books, Vancouver. Additional end matter © 2003 by Gareth Stevens, Inc.

Series editor: Lauren Fox
Design: Katherine A. Goedheer
Cover design: Renee M. Bach

Photo credits: Tim Christie 4, 20; M. Quinton/First Light 6; Thomas Kitchin/First Light 8, 18, 26, 28; Wayne Wegner/ First Light 10, 16, 30; Robert Lankinen/First Light 12; Michael Wheatley 14; Wayne Lynch 22, 24

Printed in the United States of America

1 2 3 4 5 6 7 8 9 07 06 05 04 03

# Contents

World of Difference

The bite of a beaver can topple tall trees. Using strong jaw muscles, the beaver can chomp through a trunk more than half a yard (half a meter) thick. Its four front teeth — an upper and lower pair — are built for gnawing. The teeth are long and strong and as sharp as chisels. They're always growing, and they never get dull. These amazing teeth are even protected from chipping by a hard orange coating.

Beavers are rodents — animals that have four special teeth for gnawing. The rodent family includes mice, squirrels, and porcupines. In North America, the beaver

With sharp teeth for tools, a beaver can easily cut down trees.

Beavers are well known for their dense fur and broad tails.

is the biggest member of this family. It can weigh as much as a large dog and measure about 3 feet (1 meter) long, including its tail.

Thick beaver coats range in color from yellow-brown to reddish to almost black. They are made of two different kinds of fur: long and silky, and short and woolly. The coats are always kept clean and well oiled, which helps beavers stay dry.

The wide, flat tail of a beaver has very little hair. Instead, it is covered with thick, leathery scales. A scaly tail is easier to flip around in water. The tail moves like a rudder — up and down, or side to side — whenever the beaver swims.

Don't let the little eyes, ears, and nostrils of a beaver fool you. It can see well both above and below water. Its hearing is excellent, and its sense of smell is keen.

BEAVER GIANTS

Thousands — even millions — of years ago, beavers grew as big as bears. Some were more than 8 feet (2.5 meters) long and weighed 800 pounds (360 kilograms). Along with mammoths and other giants of their time, these beavers lived in Europe, Asia, and North America. Scientists think the beavers fed on plants that grew in marshes. Some native North Americans believed that giant beavers built the continents by scooping up mud and stones from an ancient sea.

Where in the World

Beavers are at home in water close to woods. When they look for places to settle, they often head for lakes, ponds, or lazy streams with plenty of trees nearby.

Water helps protect beavers. On their stubby legs, they can't easily escape fast-running enemies, such as wolves and bears. But beavers can swim fast. By building their homes in the water or along the banks, they are never far from safety.

Woods provide most of the food beavers need, especially tree bark. They also provide the branches and twigs beavers use to build their homes, called lodges, in

Heading home to its pond, this beaver feels safest in the water.

9

Swimming over a dam is no challenge for a water expert like the beaver.

the water. If they dig out a den in a riverbank instead of building a lodge, they might use branches to cover it.

A family of beavers needs quite a large area, or territory. They may claim a stretch of shoreline more than a mile (2 kilometers) long. When young beavers grow up, they travel at least 30 miles

(50 kilometers) to find places of their own. Some have moved as far as 150 miles (250 kilometers) away from where they were born.

In North America, beavers live from the Arctic to Mexico and from the Pacific Ocean to the Atlantic. By swimming through salt water, they have even settled on many of the islands that lie along both coasts. Some beavers also live in a few parts of Europe and Asia. Although they are less common today, their numbers are still healthy.

IN THE SWIM

Strong, graceful swimmers, beavers are champions in the water. They can speed along at 5 miles (8 kilometers) per hour. Their broad, webbed back feet provide the power, while their tails do most of the steering.

When beavers dive, they close their ears and nostrils. See-through lids protect their eyes. Flaps of skin behind their big front teeth keep water out of their mouths. Beavers can stay underwater for up to fifteen minutes at a time.

11

World of the Builder

Leave it to beavers to build a great home. They often build a dam first, creating a deep pond that won't freeze to the bottom in winter. The dam might also widen the pond and make nearby trees easier to reach.

Beavers start building a dam by poking sticks into the mud beneath the water. Layer by layer, they add twigs, branches, and rocks. They also use any empty bottles or old tires that they find. Carrying, dragging, rolling, or floating their building materials, the beavers work hard to move the materials to the dam.

Finally, they scoop up mud with their handlike front paws and pack it into the

Fresh mud is great for filling cracks in a beaver lodge.

Even in snowy winters, beavers keep warm inside their lodge.

cracks. A finished dam can be more than 16 feet (5 meters) tall. The beavers work all year to keep it leakproof.

In the middle of the pond, beavers build a lodge in much the same way. Big families make big lodges, but most are about 16 feet (5 meters) wide and often rise 6 feet (2 meters) above the water.

The beavers make under-water openings in the lodge. Then they cut out one or more rooms above the water surface for gathering, eating, and sleeping. Often they blanket the floor of a sleeping area with soft layers of shredded wood.

Fresh air enters the lodge through openings in the roof. Beavers heat the lodge with their own bodies. You will know they are at home if you spot warm air rising from the top of a lodge roof on a cold day.

HOME IMPROVEMENT

Beaver dams help create more homes for many animals besides beavers. Fish and frogs move into ponds that the dams create. Mink and muskrat settle along the shore. Birds and bats skim across the water. Moose wade in to feed.

Many new plants grow where beavers have cut down trees, providing food for rabbits and deer. Even trees that die from the flooding caused by beaver dams become homes for raccoons and woodpeckers.

World Full of Food

A hungry beaver is a busy beaver. It has to gnaw trees to get its favorite food. Working mostly at night, the beaver chisels its way through a trunk, then scrambles aside to avoid the falling tree. The best parts to eat are the bark, twigs, buds, and leaves.

Beavers prefer aspen, poplar, willow, and birch trees, but they also eat other kinds of trees, including cherry and apple. Luckily for the beaver, it can use the same trees for building as it does for eating. After it strips branches and small trunks bare, it can add them to a lodge or dam.

As beavers chew down trees close to

Crack! Snap! Twigs make a fast and healthy meal.

Too hungry to wait, this beaver chows down before it gets home.

the water, they must head farther away for food. To make the job easier, they dig deep canals that may be wider than your bed and several hundred feet (hundreds of meters) long. Water from a pond, lake, or river flows through the canals, and beavers float logs, branches, and other building materials through them.

Summer provides easy-to-get treats for beavers. They nibble on grasses, berries, flowers, and most kinds of water plants. And they can be very tidy snackers. When beavers eat thick lily pads, for example, they first roll them up like tubes. They hold food in their front paws — much like you do in your hands.

Sometimes there is not enough food around — even for hardworking beavers. But they're prepared for tough times using energy from fat stored in their tails.

FOOD FROM THE ICEBOX

Each fall, northern beavers pack away food for the winter. They choose a spot in deep water close to home and pile up layers of branches. Through the winter, they visit this "icebox" whenever they need food.

Beavers may also swim beneath the ice to grab roots of cattails and other water plants. On mild winter days, they sometimes leave the water to eat. By climbing on top of deep snow, they can often chew the bark high up on tall trees.

World of Words

A tail slap can sound like a firecracker — if the tail belongs to a beaver. When they sense danger, beavers often whack their tails hard on the water. The sound can travel more than a mile (2 kilometers), warning other beavers and sometimes scaring off enemies, such as coyotes.

Tail talk is loud, but it's not the only "talking" beavers do. Young beavers — called kits — squeal softly to welcome their mothers back home. They also whine and coo in high-pitched voices, but when they want food, they g-rr-unt.

Beavers often talk to their kits by rubbing noses and making noises. All family

"Let's get out of here!" A beaver sounds an alarm by slapping the water with its tail.

The beaver has a nose for news. It smells messages left by other beavers.

members talk while they're cleaning themselves, making soft sounds.

Beavers also communicate by setting out smelly signs. Around their territory, they pile up mud and bits of plants — sometimes on top of stones. The piles may be 14 inches (35 centimeters) tall.

The beavers wet the piles with smelly oils produced by glands at their back ends.

By sniffing these signs, a beaver can tell if they were made by members of its family or not. It also knows whether the sign makers are male or female, young or old. If a male finds the smelly sign of a male from another family, he may drive the outsider away by hissing, growling, and slapping his tail. But if he discovers the signs of a female from another family, he may follow the signs to find her. She just might become his mate.

LOOKING GOOD, FEELING BETTER

Beavers have handy combs: the claws on all four feet. They comb their thick fur often to remove mats, dirt, and burrs. One claw on each of their back feet is split. This claw helps the beavers waterproof their fur, spreading oil from glands at their back ends and at the roots of their fur.

Tucked away in their dry lodges or dens, beavers often comb one another. This grooming not only helps keep their fur in good shape, it also seems to relax the beavers.

New World

Mates for now, mates forever. Most beavers choose their partners for life. Together, they build their homes, defend their territories, and raise their families.

In spring, a female beaver gives birth in her lodge or den to three or four kits. Each one is only as long as a pen and weighs about as much as a loaf of bread.

Newborn beavers are amazing. They already have teeth and furry beaver coats. They can see, and they can walk. Within a few days, kits can even swim, but they don't go past the water just below their home.

Snuggling and snoozing, the young kits spend most of their time near their mother.

Peek inside a beaver lodge and you might spot a mother with one of her kits.

Father beaver hurries home with a fresh branch for his family's lunch.

She keeps them safe and warm, and she feeds them her milk — up to nine times a day. Gradually, she adds tender twigs to their meals. Their father usually gathers and delivers food to them.

The parents also work to keep the kits' bed clean. Every one or two days, they dump the old layer of wood chips or grass into the water and replace it with fresh bedding.

Kits may be only four days old when they start to clean themselves. Still, their parents help them care for their fur.

If a beaver mother must leave her kits, older siblings often baby-sit. Beaver families usually include three or four beavers that are one to two years old. Like their parents, these baby-sitters are quick to rescue a kit that tumbles into the water. They often haul it back by the tail.

CLOSE ROOMMATES

In North America, another animal also begins life in a beaver lodge. A beaver beetle — which is smaller than this "o" — lays its eggs on the floor. When the eggs hatch, the beetles move onto a resting beaver. Tiny hooks and combs on their bodies help them cling to their furry host.

Beaver beetles spend almost all of their lives on a beaver. They feed by scraping their host's skin and dining on the oil in it. The beetles don't seem to bother the beaver much.

Small World

When it's time to explore, kits take to the water. They cling to one of their parents until they're heavy enough to practice diving. It is a skill they need to reach the underwater openings to their lodge.

At first, a parent beaver coaches its kits, swimming along beside them. If they tire, they can always get help. Some parents use their mouths to hold and push the kits. Others give them piggyback rides home.

Kits usually complete their diving lessons in one or two nights. Then they're ready to follow older beavers around, watching and imitating what they do.

Staying close to its mother, a young beaver learns to carry food through the water.

Young beavers like to have fun. What game might these three be playing?

The kits practice being adult beavers by gnawing trees and digging canals.

By fall, some kits start to help their families gather and store food underwater. Small kits may have to dive again and again before they can drag a branch down to the storage pile. It can take a full year for kits to become skilled at

30

cutting down trees and building dams.

As busy as beavers are, their life is not all work. Sometimes they float lazily down a stream on their backs, or they chase one another around, like children playing tag. Beavers of all ages seem to like swooping up and down in the water, occasionally leaping over other beavers.

By age two, most beavers are ready to leave home and start their own families. They have about ten years of busy living ahead of them.

BUSY, BUSY BEAVER

Beavers often amaze people. Here are some of the reasons why:

- **A beaver dam can be as long as 4,900 feet (1,500 meters). Some dams are strong enough for a horse to cross.**

- **When beavers gnaw down trees, they often prop themselves up on their tails.**

- **A pair of beavers can build a small dam in twenty-four hours.**

- **Beavers can cut down trees more than 100 feet (30 meters) tall.**

Glossary

canals — waterways that are made by digging. Canals help move water and materials from one place to another.

chisels — tools with sharp edges used for cutting and shaping wood.

dam — a wall or other barrier that holds back water.

den — the place where some wild animals live.

glands — parts of the body that produce fluid from materials in the bloodstream.

gnaw — to bite or chew on something and wear it away with the teeth.

mates — (n) pairs of male and female animals that produce young.

nibble — (v) to eat with small bites.

rudder — the movable part on the back of a boat used for steering.

territory — the area where animals live, mate, and search for food.

topple — to cause to fall forward or tumble over.

Index